Writing to God

Kids' Edition

Rachel G. Hackenberg

PARACLETE PRESS
BREWSTER, MASSACHUSETTS

for Noah and Faith

Acknowledgments

I am deeply grateful to all of my young friends who wrote prayers for this book. Thank you, each one of you! A special thanks to my children, Noah and Faith, who helped with edits and suggestions as I wrote. I am once again impressed by and appreciative of Jon Sweeney and the Paraclete Press team for the creative vision and editing insights that have guided this book.

Writing to God: Kids' Edition

2012 First Printing

Copyright © 2012 by Rachel Hackenberg

ISBN 978-1-61261-107-5

Scripture quotations marked NRSV are taken from the New Revised Standard Version Bible, copyright © 1989 by the Division of Christian Education of the National Council of the Churches of Christ in the United States of America, and are used by permission. All rights reserved.

All other Scripture quotations are the author's own paraphrases.

Library of Congress Cataloging-in-Publication Data
Hackenberg, Rachel G.
  Writing to God / Rachel G. Hackenberg. — Kids' ed.
      p. cm.
  ISBN 978-1-61261-107-5 (trade pbk.)
  1. Children—Prayers and devotions. 2. Spiritual journals—Authorship—Juvenile literature. I. Title.
  BV265.H23 2012
  242'.62—dc23   2011051534

10 9 8 7 6 5 4 3 2 1

Published by Paraclete Press
Brewster, Massachusetts
www.paracletepress.com

Printed in the United States of America

Hi! My name is Rachel.

When I was a girl, I wasn't sure how to pray. Should I use fancy church words?

Holy   Thee   **THOU**   *Blessed*   Trinity   Amen

Should I put my hands together and close my eyes? (Closing my eyes usually put me to sleep.) Should I pray for the whole entire world? And how could I pray for the whole entire world if I didn't know the name of every person . . . *Laboni, Dae, Aram, Vahe, Elizabeth, Paavo, Ianthe, José* . . . or the name of every place and every plant and every animal?

Most of the time, adults did the praying for me. My dad prayed at dinner. My pastor prayed during church. My teachers prayed in Sunday school. Adults wrote the books of prayer that I read in the morning before school. Adults wrote the prayers that we said aloud in church (including Jesus, who gave us the "Our Father" prayer).

So I never learned how to pray using my own words.

I just guessed.

Um ... **HI GOD.**

I felt pretty certain that my made-up prayers weren't very good and didn't really work.

...Can you hear me?

But I kept trying. I really wanted to say prayers to God using my own words, sharing my own feelings, asking my own questions.

One day—much later, when I had grown up—I was watching my baby son as he slept in his crib, and I wanted to say a special prayer that was just for him. I wanted to ask God to wrap love around him like a blanket. I decided to write down my prayer so that I could keep it and keep praying it as my son grew up.

I wrote:
May the angels guide you.
May the LORD hold you and
be with you for your whole life.

When he was a few years older, I wrote this:
God, walk beside him through the hallways at school. Sit with him in classes and in the cafeteria. Laugh with him, teach him, and bring him safely home after school.

As I looked at the words I had written, it was like all the puzzle pieces of prayer finally fit together! When I wrote down these prayers, I finally realized that I actually *could* pray. . . .

. . . and I haven't stopped writing my prayers ever since! I like to call this prayer-writing, and I use prayer-writing everywhere! I carry a pencil or pen and paper with me so that I can write prayers anytime and anywhere: at the kitchen table, in my car, just before bedtime, at my church, in the coffee shop, at a friend's house, on the beach, at the computer. Anywhere!

Today, after all these years, I can say that I love praying. I think if I had discovered prayer-writing when I was a kid, I might not have felt for such a long time that it was hard to pray.

If you feel like you don't know how to pray (like I felt when I was your age), maybe I can help! You might enjoy prayer-writing as a way to talk to God.

This book has ideas to show you how to write prayers in your own words. You can read through the whole book and try all of the ideas together, or you can try one new idea every day. You can use these ideas to write prayers with your family, or you can write prayers that are just between you and God.

Your prayers don't have to be perfect to reach God. You don't have to use big or fancy words. Your prayers can be long or short. Your prayers may even tell a story using words or pictures. Your prayers can be happy or sad or grumpy. Your prayers can have misspelled words and crossed-out words. (God understands when we make mistakes.)

Just be honest with God. Use words that make sense to you. Write about what you're feeling. Tell God when things are really great . . . and when they're not. Have fun using prayer-writing as a chance to talk to God.

And—no matter what your prayer looks like on paper—please know that God is enjoying this conversation with you!

from Rachel

Idea  Writing prayers that use your five senses.

Let's start with the *sense of sight*. What are three things that you can see, right now, where you are? Write to God and tell God something about each of these three things.

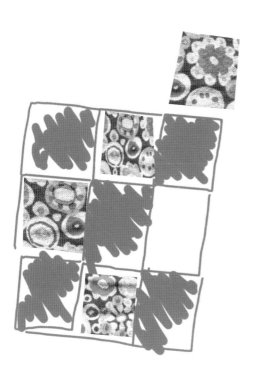

For example, I see flowers and a mirror and a pen. So I tell God:

The yellow and white flowers are beautiful.

The next time I look in that mirror,
I want to remember that God loves me.
I like to write with my favorite blue pen.

I know that those sentences don't start with "Dear God" or end with "Amen,"
but each sentence is a prayer—a short conversation with God!

Idea  Writing prayers that use your five senses.

Let's use the sense of touch next for praying. Think about holding a rock in your hand. Does it feel smooth or bumpy? Is it hard, or does it crumble easily? Is it heavy? What can you do with rocks? Write "Thank you for rocks" and then make a list of cool ways that we use rocks.

Here's my example:

Thank you for rocks
that make roads and become buildings.
Thank you for rocks that I can skip across the river.

Logan (age 5) **prays:**

Dear God, Thank you for rocks.
They are cool because . . .
they're hard
you can collect rocks
some rocks can draw
they make shapes
they can line up in a row.

Idea #1   Writing prayers that use your five senses.

How about the *sense of hearing*? Do you ever hear bad news? Sometimes we hear something sad or scary or mean when we're listening to people talk around us, listening to the radio or television. Tell God about some bad news that you've heard.

I want to tell God:

I'm so sad to hear that my grandfather is sick. I'm worried because he is in the hospital. Would you please take care of him, and take care of my grandmother, and of me too?

Emily (age 12) prays:

Dear Lord, I woke up this morning full of life, and five seconds later my world went up in smoke. I couldn't bear the words I was hearing. My sister is moving! Pull me through this, Lord. Let me know I am loved . . .

 **Idea #1**

Writing prayers that use your five senses.

Now the *sense of taste!* You can probably think quickly of foods that you love to taste. Did you know that there's a Bible verse that says, "Taste and see that the Lᴏʀᴅ is good!" (Psalm 34:8, ɴʀsᴠ)? This verse tells us that we can use all of our senses—even taste—to get to know God. How awesome that even the food we eat can remind us of God! Write or draw pictures of food that you like (and food that you don't like!) to thank God for the different kinds of food in the world.

I thank God for:

warm tomato soup on a chilly day

lima beans (even though I think they are really gross)

corn-on-the-cob with butter

apples (God, it's amazing that you can make one little apple seed grow into a whole apple tree with new apples!)

Writing prayers that use your five senses.

Finally, the *sense of smell.* I wonder how our noses and brains decide if things smell good or nasty. Or why some people like a smell that other people dislike. God is amazing for creating so many scents! Write to God about the things you smell.

These are some of the things that I am thankful for smelling, God:

chocolate cookies baking in the oven
a hamster cage that needs to be cleaned
the kind-of-good, kind-of-stinky smell of mud after rain
smoke from a campfire

This list doesn't look like a prayer,

but I thank God for the sense of

smell to experience the odors of life!

Idea #2 Writing to God about your feelings.

Write to God when you're upset about something you shouldn't have done (or something you *should* have done but didn't do). Start with "I'm sorry."

One summer, I was angry at my friend Alexi. I thought Alexi was ignoring me, so I decided to ignore her too. We didn't speak all summer. Then she called me one day . . . and I realized that I had been a bad friend to her! I wrote this prayer after we talked:

I'm sorry that I hurt Alexi's feelings by ignoring her. I was wrong to be angry. Please help me forget my anger.

An "I'm sorry" prayer from Logan (age 7):

Dear God: I'm sorry that I was not being a good friend to my Nana. That I was not being a good sport. I know that you want me to be good. I played another game with her and didn't call her a cheater. When I make bad choices, it makes people feel bad. I will try to be better.

Idea #2 Writing to God about your feelings.

What do you say when something great happens? I hear kids say things like "Wow!" "Cool!" "That rocks." "Awesome!" and "OMG!" Write to God when you feel surprised or amazed by something great that happens. Start your prayer with "Wow, God!"

Sometimes in the morning I want to tell God:

Wow! That sunrise was awesome!

When I'm at the ocean, I often pray:

God, the sound of waves crashing on the beach is so cool!

Noah (age 11) writes:

Wow, God, something amazing just happened:
Francesca learned how to ride a scooter!
It made me feel so happy because
me and Faith taught her how.

Idea #2 Writing to God about your feelings.

God knows that sometimes we feel tired, sometimes our bodies hurt, sometimes we feel grumpy about being ourselves and we want to be more like someone else. Tell God about those feelings.

When I go somewhere and there are people I don't know, I feel very nervous.

I worry that people won't like me. One time, I wrote this prayer:

I'm not perfect, God. There are lots of things
I don't know how to do. I don't like it when
people look at me funny. But you made me,
God, and you love me.

Madison (age 7) prays about her feelings:

Dear God, I feel angry when my siblings
do something to make me mad.
Help them to not make me mad. Amen.

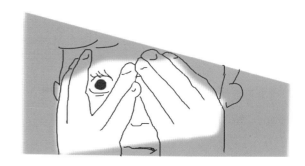

Idea

Writing to God about your feelings.

Everyone gets scared sometimes. What scares you? When I was your age, I had nightmares that scared me during the night. (I'm still a little scared of the dark.) Try writing to God when you feel scared.

After everyone at my house goes to sleep at night (everyone except me!), I can hear strange noises around my house: creaks from the stairs, mice running in the attic, and imaginary noises that my mind invents! Telling God about it helps me feel better:

The middle of the night scares me
when all the lights are out and everything's quiet.
God, please help me sleep even though I'm scared.

Ashley (age 11) prays:

Dear God, sometimes I get scared
when I am by myself and when
I am sleeping all by myself in my bed.
I am also scared if my mom
and dad aren't home.
Please keep me protected from bad people.

Idea #2
Writing to God about your feelings.

Tell God when you're happy. God likes to hear your joy! You can write sentences about feeling happy, or write a list of things that make you happy. For example, I'm happy about:

eating ice cream

watching funny cartoons with my kids

VACATION!

hiking a mountain

listening to a Beethoven symphony

feeling the wind of a thunderstorm

FAMILY

reading a book

SUNFLOWERS

hearing music from cars driving by

CHOCOLATE

Here's one more example: every year when autumn comes to Pennsylvania (where I live), I tell God that I'm happy for the return of fall.

Seeing the cloudless blue sky in October
and taking a walk through crunching leaves
makes me feel so happy, God!

Logan (age 5) **writes:**

Dear God,
I thank you for making me happy.
I'm happy you . . .
made my parents this way
let me play soccer on a team
made the Wii
had my mom have a baby girl
let me have sisters and brothers
made chips because I really like chips
made medicine for my brother to help him.

Idea #3 Writing prayers using Bible verses.

Psalm 103 begins, "Bless the Lord, O my soul" (NRSV). *Bless* is a word that we read a lot in the Bible; to bless means to do something good and helpful for someone else. *O my soul* means that the writer is talking to himself. So in this verse, the writer is telling himself to do something good for God. Can we do good things that help God? Write a prayer about ways that you can help God.

I wrote this prayer:

God,
today I'm going to smile at you like a sunny dandelion;
I'm going to get out my crayons and make a drawing
for your refrigerator; then I'm going to sit quietly and listen to you,
just in case you want to talk to somebody.

Idea #3 Writing prayers using Bible verses.

Isaiah 11:6–8 says, "The wolf will live peacefully next to the lamb. The cow and the bear will eat grass in the same field. The calf and the cub will sleep next to each other. A crawling baby will play safely near a snake's den." Isaiah imagines a world that seems impossible! A hungry wolf doesn't eat a little lamb? A baby isn't hurt by poisonous snakes? Can you believe it? Can you imagine a world so peaceful that even predator animals get along with their prey? Isaiah says that this impossible peace can happen when the whole earth knows God. Write a prayer about peace, and about getting along with others.

Kayli (age 10) prays for peace with her sister and brother:

Dear God, please help me get along with others.
Help me have peace between me and my siblings. I need to remember that Isaiah imagines a world where predators get along with their prey. Help me get along with everyone like that. Amen.

Andrew (age 14) writes this prayer:

Lord, as I walked down the street this morning I saw two men fighting about a parking spot. I saw a woman hit her dog for not listening. I heard more news about all the countries that are fighting. As I look at all the unpeaceful things that happen, I hope and pray that you help me to see more peace in my everyday life. I also ask that you give this world more opportunities to make peace, and not just for me but for everyone treated unequally and for all this useless fighting in the world, Lord. Please save us.

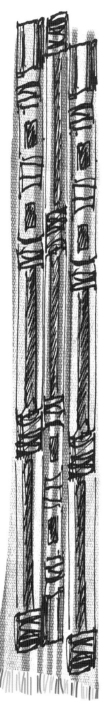

Idea #3 Writing prayers using Bible verses.

Psalm 150:3–4 is a song: "Celebrate God with sounds from a trumpet, a guitar and a harp! Celebrate God with tambourines shaking and feet dancing! Celebrate God with fiddle and flute!" Do you have a favorite song? Can you sing it out loud to God? (Or make up your own song for God!)

I'm going to invent my song to the tune of the ABCs, and sing:

I love God
and God loves me,
so I sing my song with glee!
When the strong wind blows the trees,
I just smile and twirl with ease!
I love God and God loves me,
so I sing my song with glee!

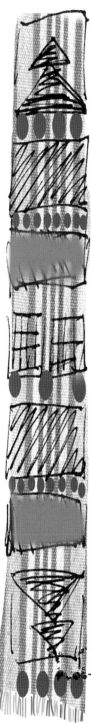

Idea #3 Writing prayers using Bible verses.

There's a story in John 21: "Seven friends were fishing at sea one night, all through the night. In the morning when they returned to shore, Jesus was there with a campfire on the beach. Fresh fish was cooking on the fire, and there was bread too. Jesus invited them to eat breakfast." Did you know that Jesus could cook? Imagine that Jesus is cooking breakfast for you, and tell him about your day today while you wait for breakfast.

For example:

Good morning, Jesus. Today I have chores (I have to clean my room!), but then I want to play outside with my friends or maybe read a book.

Dante (age 7) tells Jesus about his day:

Morning, Jesus. Today I get to go to my club! I want to be the club manager but I'm not . . . can you help? Amen.

Idea #3 Writing prayers using Bible verses.

John 11:35 is one of the shortest verses in the Bible. It just says, "Jesus cried." Have you ever thought about Jesus crying? In John 11:35, Jesus cries because his friend Lazarus has died, and he cries because he's sad to see Mary and Martha crying. God gets sad when people are hurting or crying . . . and God hears us when we're sad. Write to God about crying.

I don't often cry in front of other people. One day I wrote this prayer after I closed my bedroom door:

Jesus, do you hear me crying
when I hide my tears in the pillow?

Elene (age 5) prays:

Dear God, you know how I almost fell off my bike the other day? Remember when I was riding home from Chris's house? It was getting dark so I rode my bike very fast to get home. Did you know how scared I was? Really scared! So scared I was crying. Love, Elene

Idea #4 Writing to God about nature.

Water is all around us! There is water in the air we breathe. We use water to wash our faces and brush our teeth. We see water in rivers and in icicles and fog. It's amazing how many forms of water God made, and how many ways we use water! Choose a form of water—such as clouds, snow, rain puddles, ocean, or ice—and write to God about it!

I like to watch thunderstorm clouds moving across the sky. Even though God knows all about clouds (because God made the clouds!), I still like to describe the clouds to God. I want God to know that I'm paying attention to God's work in nature.

> When I see the thunderstorm clouds coming near my house, they are both beautiful and frightening.
> The clouds are bulging with rain, they are enormous, and they have dark shades of gray.

Eric (age 6, almost 7) writes this prayer about water:

> To my friend God,
> God you were a good thinker
> when you thought of making water for us.
> I thank you for making water, because the
> water you made can turn into ice and my
> mommy lets me have ice water every night
> before I say prayers to you. Thank you God
> for making cold and hot water that can
> also turn into ice. Amen.

Idea #4 Writing to God about nature.

Can you see a tree right now? Do its branches reach high like a sycamore tree, or do they spread out wide like a Christmas pine tree? Is it a tree that you could climb, like Zacchaeus once climbed a tree so that he could see Jesus? Is it a fruit tree? You know, Jesus and his friends picked fruit from trees (like figs) to eat as they walked from town to town. Write to God about trees. You might tell God what you like about trees, or ask God a question about trees.

For example, when I look at really tall trees, I want to ask God:

If I could stand as tall as a sequoia tree,
would you see me better?

I bet that God watched me climb trees when I was a kid.

That makes me think of another prayer:

> God, thank you for the strong maple tree
> that I used to climb to the tippy-top (and thank
> you for keeping me safe as I climbed).

Idea #4 Writing to God about nature.

God takes care of the creatures of the world—from the crawling beetle to the colorful hoopoe bird to the impressive blue whale. Jesus told us that God even knows if a sparrow falls. Do you have a pet at home? Write a prayer for your pet. (Or if you don't have a pet, write a prayer for the animals, birds, or bugs that live outside.)

We don't have pets at my home, but there are squirrels *everywhere*

outside my house, and it's funny to watch them chase each other.

One day, I wrote this prayer:

The squirrels make me laugh, God,
when they play tag around the tree trunk.
Please keep them safe when they leap
through the tree branches.

A.J. (age 7) **prays:**

Dear God, bless
Shelly my hermit crab
and keep him safe as
he crawls around his
little cage.

Idea #4 Writing to God about nature.

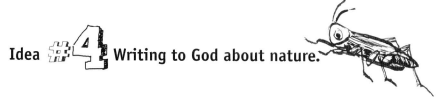

Nature is full of the color green! There are green pine needles, green grasses, green frogs, green parakeets, and green grasshoppers. In plants, green is caused by *chlorophyll,* a chemical that helps the plants gather sunlight to grow. Even with the same chemical, every green is a little bit different. Tell God about the shades of green that you see.

I see:
the shiny lime green of poison ivy leaves,
dark jade of a Norway spruce tree,
olive green grass in the yard,
the blue-green of tall onion grass sprinkled with dew drops,
and the soft emerald of an iris flower's stem.

God made so many beautiful shades of green!

Idea #4 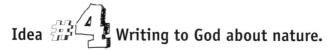 Writing to God about nature.

One tiny ant has the strength to pick up sticks and food crumbs that weigh as much as twenty ants. That might not sound like much—you could hold twenty ants in your hand and they wouldn't be too heavy—but can you imagine having the strength to carry twenty kids? What do you need extra strength to do? Tell God!

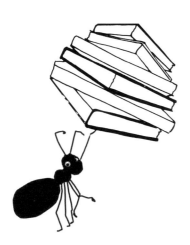

Here are some ways that I pray for extra strength:

I need energy today to play a soccer game.

or

God, I need extra strength to be
nice to Rebecca today
even though she was mean to
me yesterday.

or

School is really long today and I
don't have lunch until 1:00.
Please make the time go fast so
that I can eat and feel strong for
the rest of my classes.

Idea #5 Writing to God about ordinary events in your life.

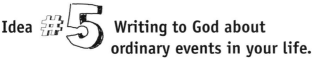

God knows what happens to us, but it's important to tell God about our lives too. As we talk to God, we remember that God loves us. Also, talking to God reminds us that we're not alone. Let's start Idea #5 by thinking about something ordinary (but sometimes painful!) that happens to all of us: falling down. Have you ever tripped or slid or fainted or tumbled? Tell God about a time when you fell down.

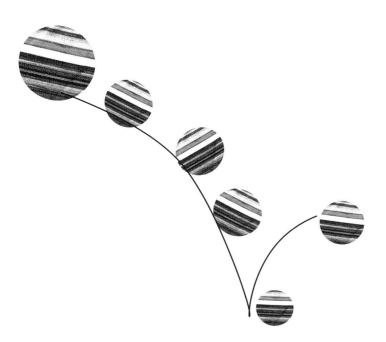

When I was in school, there was an afternoon when I was riding bikes with a friend. My bike bumped into a curb, and I fell down:

I still have a scar from the summer day

when I fell off my bike
— really hard —
and my knee was bleeding,
but I got back on my bike
so that no one would know how much it hurt.
Do you remember that day, God?

I like to remember a verse in Psalm 145:

"God holds onto those who fall,

and God lifts up those who

have been knocked down."

Addie (age 5½) writes this about God:

He lifts me up so I never fall,
he helps me because I'm so small.

Idea  Writing to God about ordinary events in your life.

Do you like waking up in the mornings? Do you jump out of bed with excitement for the day, or are you still sleepy even after you get dressed and eat breakfast? The writer of Psalm 108:1–4 loves to wake up for another day of singing songs to God. (He even wants to start singing songs before dawn! "I will wake up the dawn with music. I will give thanks for God's love, which is more beautiful than the sunrise!") Tell God something about waking up.

My prayers about waking up change a lot!

Sometimes I'm tired in the morning:

God, do you ever want to sleep in
in the mornings? I do!

Sometimes I like to wake up early to listen to the quiet:

It's so nice to sit still, God, before the day gets busy.
I can hear a bird, just starting to wake up and sing.
Everything else is quiet, and I just sit and listen to the bird's song.

Sometimes the day is busy, so I wake up very quickly:

Good morning, God! I have so much to do today,
but thank you for the cool morning breeze that makes me smile
as I hurry up into the day.

Idea #5  Writing to God about ordinary events in your life.

Here's something that we all do: we travel! Some of us travel by taking a walk down the block to the store. Some of us travel by flying in an airplane to another country. Some of us travel by driving in a car to church or school. In the Bible, especially the Old Testament, there are stories about God traveling with people no matter where they go. Make a list of places you've traveled to (like Grandma's house, Disney World, Lake Michigan). Choose one place from your list, and tell God about traveling there.

Here's my story about traveling:

When we drove through North Carolina, God,
it rained the whole time. I was scared,
because the storm was so much bigger than our car,
but you stayed with us and kept us safe!

This is a trip that I take often, and I say this prayer each time:

Thank you for Grandma and Grandpa's house.
Thank you for their big brown chairs that I can curl up in.
Thank you for the love that I feel when I'm there.
God, thank you for your love that is there!

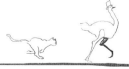

Idea #5 Writing to God about ordinary events in your life.

Let's talk to God about school. What grade are you in? What do you enjoy learning about? What is hard to learn? My favorite classes in school were math and reading. I had trouble learning and remembering places (like the capital city of a state, or the location of a country on a map). Do you ever ask God for help when you want to do your best in school or on a test? Tell God about school.

When I was worried about a test at school, I would pray a very short prayer:

Dear God,
help!

I also write prayers when
I want to learn more about God:

Teach me to understand
that you care about everybody.
Teach me to live each day
by loving others and showing
kindness.

Faith (age 9) tells God:

In school I like art class. It gives
me time to draw, and I want to
be an artist when I grow up.

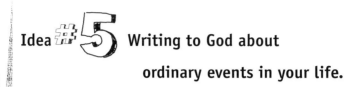

Idea #5 Writing to God about ordinary events in your life.

Sometimes we say prayers to tell God about things that happen, and sometimes we say prayers to tell God about things that *don't* happen. For example, my daughter likes to be in the same class at school as her best friend, but last year they were in different classes. The thing she wanted to happen didn't happen, and she was disappointed. Here's another example: My children really wanted a pet, but I didn't want one. One evening, we went to a carnival to play games, and my kids won a goldfish! Something that I didn't expect to happen, happened anyway! Write a prayer about something that didn't happen.

Once I was having a very busy day, and I was late to a meeting. When I got there, it turned out that the meeting had been canceled! I was very glad that it didn't happen, and I took a minute to write this prayer:

> God, I'm so glad that this meeting didn't happen.
> Thank you for giving me a minute to slow down
> and take a deep breath on this busy day.

Samuel (age 8) tells God:

Dear God: I would like two new sisters.

Jelisa (age 10) writes to God:

Dear Lord, I wanted to be there with Aunt Sara two days before she died, but I couldn't because I had to go to school and take care of family. My Aunt Sara was special to me; even though she was sick she bought me clothes and toys. Thank you for everything. In Jesus' name, amen.

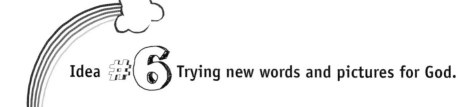

Idea #6 Trying new words and pictures for God.

What's your favorite color? What do you like about that color? As you think about your favorite color, can you imagine anything that God has in common with that color? For example, if you like blue because it's a beautiful color for the sky, you could say that blue is beautiful . . . and God is beautiful too! Describe how God is like your favorite color.

For example, I like the color yellow:

>yellow is sunny . . . so is God

>yellow makes me feel happy . . . just like God

>sometimes yellow is hard to see (like in a rainbow) . . .

>and sometimes I have trouble seeing God too

Faith (age 9) likes lime green:

Lime green is my favorite color because it's bright, and it's a cool color. I think that God is bright, and God is very cool.

Idea #6 Try new words and pictures for God.

Use the weather outside to help you write a prayer. Is it raining right now? Is the sun shining? Is it hot? Is there snow falling onto the sidewalk? Whatever the weather is doing today, try asking God to do that too!

On a rainy day, I might pray:

Rain on me, God, get me soaking wet
to clean me and help me grow.

On a cold and frosty morning, I write to God:

Cover me, God,
like the frost covers the ground.

Watching clouds move across the sky on a windy day, I pray:

Blow on me like the wind. Mold me, like you mold the clouds into
many shapes.

Idea #6 Try new words and pictures for God.

Jesus described himself in funny ways, sometimes. In the Gospel of John, Jesus said: "I am the bread. I am the light. I am the gate. I am the shepherd. I am the vine." These are ordinary things (bread, light, gate, shepherd, vine), but Jesus used them to give us ideas about who he is. Let's use ordinary things to find ideas about God. Write a sentence to describe something that you use every day. Then put the word "God" into that sentence. How does it sound? Does it teach you anything new about God, or give you new ideas for a prayer?

For example, I'll describe a plate:

The plate is flat and blue; the plate holds food
and brings me together with other people.

Now I'll write "God" instead of "plate":

God is flat and blue; God holds food
and brings me together with other people.

Okay, this prayer is a little silly—I
don't think God is flat and blue—but it
reminds me that God provides food and
brings us together!

Idea #6 Try new words and pictures for God.

When life gets really busy, or when we feel afraid and confused, Psalm 46:10 tells us to quiet down and spend time thinking about God. "Be still and know that I am God" (NRSV). Put this book down, sit still, and just listen to your breathing. Imagine that God is as close to you as your breath.

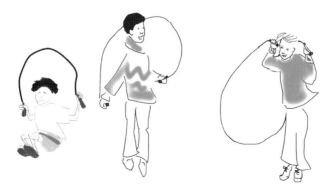

You can think about these phrases as you imagine God in your breath:

(breathing in) God loves me.
(breathing out) I am God's child.

Have you ever had trouble breathing? Maybe you had a piece of food stuck in your throat, maybe you had an asthma attack, maybe you were running and had trouble catching your breath. You can write a prayer to the Holy Spirit (often called God's breath) about your breathing, like this:

Fill up my lungs, Holy Spirit,
with oxygen for my body and with energy for today.

Idea #6 Try new words and pictures for God.

Choose a family member, someone you enjoy being around (like a grandparent, a cousin, a dad, an aunt or an uncle). Describe what you like about that person . . . but say it about God.

Thinking about my mom, for example, I write this about God:

I love God's hugs.
I love God's homemade applesauce.
I love that God tells me I'm special.

Addison (age 5½) **writes:**

I love God because
He laughs with me
He plays all my favorite games
He teaches me how to dance
He snuggles me
He kisses my boo-boos
He is my best friend.

Idea Telling God "thank you."

Psalm 92 begins, "It is good to say 'thank you' to
God every morning and every night. I will even
sing my thanksgiving with the music of a
guitar, because I am so glad that God loves
me forever!" Saying "thank you" to God
is an important part of prayer. It's a way
for us to tell God that we notice how
God loves us and takes care of us. Write
to God to say "thank you" for people who
help you and take care of you.

Here are three of my "thank you" prayers
for people who take care of me:

Thank you so much for Mom & Dad
who encourage me when I try new things.

Thank you, God, for David in New York
who teaches me about
loving you and loving everybody.

Thank you for Naomi in Washington
who makes me laugh and listens when I cry.

Idea  Tell God "thank you."

In the stories of the Bible, people
sleep in some unexpected places!
David spends many nights sleeping in
caves. Jacob goes to sleep with a rock for
his pillow one night. Jonah sleeps in the belly
of a whale. Elijah sleeps under a broom tree in the desert.

Jesus falls asleep on a boat. Where do you sleep?
Write to God to say "thank you" for the place that you sleep.

I'm thankful for:
the soft blue blankets that keep me warm,
and the pillows that I rest my head on

Jada (age 8) **writes to God:**
Dear Lord, thank you for my room and everything in it.
Thank you for the bed that I sleep on. Thank you for my closet
full of clothes. Thank you for my dresser that when I feel sleepy
I can put my books there. And most of all thank you for my sister
that when I am scared she comforts me. I am glad that you made
her and my precious room. In Jesus' name. Amen.

Idea #7  Tell God "thank you."

It's good to thank God for the food that we eat every day! We also thank God for the people who make our food. Think about your favorite snack food. Can you imagine all of the steps that it took to make that snack? For example, if your favorite snack is sweet, then someone had to cut down the sugar canes to make the sugar for your sweet snack. Thank God for your favorite snack and for the many people who help make it.

Here's my "thank you" prayer for a snack:

Mmmm, God, salt-and-vinegar chips make my tongue tingle!
I couldn't have these chips to eat without the work of
    someone planting potatoes in the ground,
      someone harvesting potatoes,
        someone cutting and cooking the potatoes,
          someone making the machine to put the chips into bags,
          and someone else to drive the chips to a grocery store.
            God, I don't know the names of these people who
             made my chips but thank you for each person.
             And thank you for chips.

71

Idea  #7 Tell God "thank you."

Let's thank God for our bodies. After all, without bodies, how would we walk or swim or sing or write prayers or smile or jump rope or sneeze or sleep? I know that sometimes our bodies get sick, or we break a leg, or a part of the body doesn't work (like when someone's ears cannot hear). Still, we need our bodies to live! Write a prayer thanking God for your body.

Here's a prayer that's specifically about toes:

My toes are funny-looking, God,
but thank you for putting toes on my feet
to help me stand and balance and walk.

This is a prayer about hands:

Thank you for children's dirty hands that have played in mud
(and thank you for soap to wash them off).
Thank you for hands holding other hands,
a gesture of people showing love and care.

Noah (age 11) writes this "thank you"

prayer about the brain:

Thank you God
for our brains.
They help us to learn,
talk,
walk,
and to control our bodies.
Without the brain,
we wouldn't have
the things we do today
(like technology and stuff).

Idea #7 Tell God "thank you."

Do you know all of the constellations of stars in the sky? I don't! Do you know all of the rivers on the earth? Me neither! Do you know how the hawk knows how to fly? That will always be a mystery to me! Sometimes I get frustrated by what I don't know, but then I like to remember that God knows everything. Write to God to say "thank you" for things that you don't know.

Looking at the sky at night, I realize how much I don't know about the universe:

God, the stars are amazing—I can see so many in the sky!
(Some stars are bright, and some are faint like freckles.)
I know there are more stars that I can't see! There are stars and planets
and galaxies that I've never heard of, and it astonishes me to imagine it!
Thank you for everything in the sky that I don't even know!

I pray this prayer almost every morning:

Dear God, thank you for this new day.
You know that I have written down my plans for today,
but we both know that plans change. I don't really know
what might happen today.
So please be with me, and thank you.

When you reach the end of *Writing to God: Kids' Edition*, you're not done praying! You can keep writing prayers to God. All you need is paper and a pencil or pen. You can reuse the ideas in this book, or even create your own ideas for prayers. You can keep a notebook full of prayers, or you might use these ideas to pray out loud with an adult. Remember that it's most important to keep talking to God (and keep listening too).

Your conversations with God will continue as you grow up. You'll learn new things. You'll have new experiences. You'll meet new people and visit new places. No matter how much things change, you can always tell God.

So just grab a pencil! God is there to listen and to love you.

About Paraclete Press

WHO WE ARE

Paraclete Press is a publisher of books, recordings, and DVDs on Christian spirituality. Our publishing represents a full expression of Christian belief and practice—from Catholic to Evangelical, from Protestant to Orthodox.

We are the publishing arm of the Community of Jesus, an ecumenical monastic community in the Benedictine tradition. As such, we are uniquely positioned in the marketplace without connection to a large corporation and with informal relationships to many branches and denominations of faith.

WHAT WE ARE DOING

BOOKS Paraclete publishes books that show the richness and depth of what it means to be Christian. Although Benedictine spirituality is at the heart of all that we do, we publish books that reflect the Christian experience across many cultures, time periods, and houses of worship. We publish books that nourish the vibrant life of the church and its people—books about spiritual practice, formation, history, ideas, and customs.

We have several different series, including the best-selling Paraclete Essentials and Paraclete Giants series of classic texts in contemporary English; A Voice from the Monastery—men and women monastics writing about living a spiritual life today; award-winning poetry; best-selling gift books for children on the occasions of baptism and first communion; and the Active Prayer Series that brings creativity and liveliness to any life of prayer.

RECORDINGS From Gregorian chant to contemporary American choral works, our music recordings celebrate sacred choral music through the centuries. Paraclete distributes the recordings of the internationally acclaimed choir Gloriæ Dei Cantores, praised for their "rapt and fathomless spiritual intensity" by *American Record Guide,* and the Gloriæ Dei Cantores Schola, which specializes in the study and performance of Gregorian chant. Paraclete is also the exclusive North American distributor of the recordings of the Monastic Choir of St. Peter's Abbey in Solesmes, France, long considered to be a leading authority on Gregorian chant.

DVDS Our DVDs offer spiritual help, healing, and biblical guidance for life issues: grief and loss, marriage, forgiveness, anger management, facing death, and spiritual formation.

LEARN MORE ABOUT US AT OUR WEBSITE:

www.paracletepress.com, or call us toll-free at 1-800-451-5006.

You may also be interested in . . .

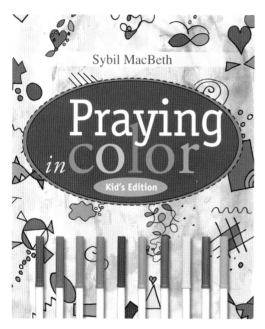

Praying in Color
Kid's Edition
Sybil MacBeth

$16.99
Oversize Paperback
ISBN: 978-1-55725-595-2

Praise for *Praying in Color*

"Just as Julia Cameron, in *The Artist's Way*, showed the hardened Harvard businessman he had a creative artist lurking within, MacBeth makes it astonishingly clear that anyone with a box of colors and some paper can have a conversation with God."
Publishers Weekly, starred review

This first-of-its-kind resource has changed the way that kids pray—and how adults teach them to do it. With *Praying in Color: Kids' Edition,* prayer makes sense to kids. One minute a day will do. Any time of the day will work. Drawing with markers or crayons is half the prayer; the other half is carrying the visual memories throughout the day.

Available from most booksellers or through Paraclete Press: www.paracletepress.com; 1-800-451-5006. Try your local bookstore first.